**Learning is like rowing against the current.
If you stop, you drift back. (Laotse)**

Ergo, give your life always a new tune...

Regina Lahner

New Meditations Made Easy

With Singing Bowls

New Proven Texts
Instantly Applicable in Practice
For Individual- and Group-Work

Cover design: Friedrich G. M. Roedig, Salzburg

Resources: Own & stock.xchng® vi www.sxc.hu

Image of Regina Lahner: Marisa Giannino, Foto Frenzel, Ulm

Lectorates: Senta Konopke und Anna Lahner

Translator: Dr. Georg Woodman, PhD, Dr. MSc., Dr. Phil., University CA/USA

Bibliographic Information: Deutsche Nationalbibliothek
Original edition: German

ISBN: 978-3-7431-9650-6
1. Edition in English 2017   © 2017 Regina Lahner

Production & publication: BoD Books on Demand, Norderstedt

Important Notice: The texts and instructions given in this book are carefully compiled and written to the best of my knowledge and belief exclude author and publisher from any liability, by the application or utilization of the here described meditations arise directly or indirectly to the user or third parties. Whether a person is with his feelings or states for a meditation lies in its sole discretion and own responsibility. By all kinds of health disorders or diseases, especially in severe or chronic, for longer lasting or even with worsening symptoms, we strongly recommend a doctor or medical practitioner should be consulted.

About the author: Regina Lahner was born in 1965 in Mönchengladbach/Germany. She's been living since her age of 2 in Bavaria/Germany and occupied herself early on in life with natural healing and all health-related topics. In 2000 she underwent an education-program of 1 year as a Dr. Edward Bach Flower Essence Remedies Therapist. Later on she worked independently in the field of advice, education and seminars, and since 2005 she's offered a distant-study program of 10 months to become a Dr. Bach Flower Essence Remedies Therapist. In the same year she accomplished her education „Tibetan Sound-Bowl-Massage" at the Sebastian-Kneipp-School in Bad Wörishofen. As a referent and seminar-chair in the field of Dr. Bach Flower Essence Remedies (speeches/workshops) and singing-bowls (courses, workshops, meditation, and creational sound-painting) Mrs. Lahner is active at numerous public schools in South-Bavaria.
2012 appeared her first book "Klangschalenmassage leicht gemacht" (Sound Massage With Singing Bowls Easy Done) and 2013 with the same publisher "Meditationen mit Klangschalen leicht gemacht" (Meditation Made Easy With Singing Bowls). Both are also published in English. 2015 appeared "Neue Meditationen mit Klangschalen leicht gemacht" and this book is the translation of it. For some years now Mrs. Lahner teaches interested persons through intensive-seminars to become Singing-Bowl Sound-Massagists.

Detailed information can be retrieved via www.bluetenberatung.de and www.tibetische-klangschalen-massage.de

Table of Contents

Preface	8
Short, practical Introduction	9
Autumn's Magic Sensory Journey	11
Stroll in the Vineyard	15
Sound Meditation at the Fireplace	21
Magic of Christmas	24
Snowflake Meditation	29
„Dreamboat" - Pair - Meditation	34
Magic Moments	40
Moments of Happiness	44
Star - Magic	48
Dream of Hawaii	52
Discover Your Inner Beauty	60
Dutch Sea of Tulips	64
We Embrace Spring	69
Enchanting Spring Awakening	73
Indian Nights	78

In the Land of the Pharaohs	82
Forest-walk: Oasis in Everyday-Life	86
The Tree of Life	92
The Cave of the Sparkling Crystals	98
QR Code for more Information	104

Preface

After my (second) german book "Meditationen mit Klangschalen leicht gemacht" (Meditation Made Easy With Singing Bowls) I received a lot of praise and I always got inquiries as to whether there was a continuation and when new text templates would appear ... That is why I once again started to work and this book for you to write.

Since it is now Volume II, I won't need to go into the preparation and realization of a sound meditation here, but only restrict myself to the pure text-pages!

I wish you a lot of fun and pleasure in the practical trial, implementation, modification and application of the texts.

Notice:
As in the past, you are allowed to use all my texts in the private sphere without restriction. You can also use the meditations in your courses and events.

However, I always ask for the necessary reference to me as a legal author in commercial use.
But, in case of any use in a printed form, I kindly request written permission in advance.
(Copyright!)

Short, practical Introduction:

For a guided meditation (with text) you should have at least 3-5 Singing Bowls. All of these bowls must be acoustically coordinated to each other! Two harmonious dark tones that "run" like a slow heart-beat through the whole meditation, plus the addition of one or more matching tones are very nice. To "wake up" you should then also use a small bowl or a cymbal with a light tone.

In the following texts I have always used blank lines which are intended to visually indicate a brief pause during reading. A larger distance therefore means a longer break!

You can, of course, also touch the Singing Bowls during this reading pause. Let them sound long - but do not wait until they have completely sounded off.

To finish the meditation, use the bowl with the brightest sound, strike it 3 times in succession with increasing intensity using a small wooden clapper (softly, gently!).

You will find many practical applications as well as the basics of the sound massage in my first book: "Sound Massage With Singing Bowls Easy Done".

Tip:

I basically do NOT use background music in the individual meditations.

In some meditations, however, I have given you a suitable music recommendation, since these can significantly support the imagination and relaxation.

These individual titles should then be used in the speech pauses and without the striking of the sound shells, so to speak as an interlude.

When using these pieces please also consider the GEMA-application you may perhaps need.

To almost every meditation -in my opinion- is very suitable the CD: "Birdsong without Music - Summer Day in the Forest" (= German Edition "Vogelgezwitscher ohne Musik – Sommertag im Wald")
by Thomas Rettenmaier (Delta Music)
ASIN: B003S5FQL2

This is available at
www.entspannungstechniken.eu
or www.Amazon.de

You can hear just soothing bird chirping!

Autumn's Magic Sensory Journey

I would like to welcome you here today very warmly to our journey of "Autumn Magic" and wish you a nice rest.

In order to find you in a relaxed state, I will address you in the following meditation by your first-name.

Make yourself now quite comfy on your exercise-mat.

Concentrate now on my voice and on your own breathing rhythm.

Feel the way of your breath for a few breaths.

Feel, how the air enters through your nose or mouth into your body,

how it fills your lungs and your abdomen,

and how it leaves your body as you exhale.

Perhaps you can also already feel how peace and serenity in your inner life ever more and more want to spread.

Your body is now quite heavy and sinks deeper and deeper into your mat.

You are beautifully warm and you feel completely comfortable, calm and perfectly relaxed.

You will soon imagine how you are taking a relaxing walk in nature on a beautiful warm day in the autumn.

The meadows and forests are bathed in deep golden light.

You walk a small dirt road away from the daily trouble and enjoy the silence of nature and the soft chirping of the birds.

Everywhere you can discover warm, bright colors.

You take each of these colors deep into your inner being and fill yourself with energy.

You'll now see:

brown shining chestnuts,

golden colored leaves,

dark verdant moss,

red and white toadstool mushrooms,

ripe yellow corn cobs,

and dark red rose hips...

You can literally feel the joy of life, which is now growing in intensity, becoming more and more intensive.

And you are looking forward to the quieter time that now comes:

on the gentle fog of the fields in the early morning,

on the last warm sunny days,

on the shining spider webs in the bushes and trees,

on the beautiful, luminous sunsets,

on the warm tea after a walk,

on the cuddly evenings by candlelight.

You can hear the soft bells from afar,

you feel a sense of security.

You taste the warm tea in your mouth,

you see a flickering candle before your mind's eye.

And you recharge your internal battery with all these impressions now...

But gradually it is time to slowly leave the magic of the autumn and return to the here and now.

Now take a deep breath.

You let your breathing rhythm become more intense again.

Your breath adapts to your normal tempo.

You start to move.

Your hands clench to fists.

You stretch and stretch, your whole body now.

You have returned to the present and feel very well.

Stroll in the Vineyard

I welcome you to our meditation "Stroll in the Vineyard" and wish you a nice relaxing.

In the following meditation, I will address you directly by your first-names in order to raise your subconscious mind even more deeply.

While you are now making yourself comfortable on your mat, your mind slowly drifts into a pleasant and relaxed state with every breath.

You can feel your belly gently rising and lowering,

as the breath streams into and out from your lungs,

and how you easily sink into your exercise-mat.

You are warm, and feel very comfortable.

All the thoughts that may now go through your mind, become less and less.

They are dissolving now - or just in a few minutes.

And now you go mentally slowly through your body.

You start at the bottom of your feet and feel,
if you can sense some tension.

You are now trying intentionally sending your breath
to your feet.

Then you go with your thoughts a bit higher,

along your calves,

to your thighs,

and now you feel inside of your pelvis.

And again, you send your breath to where you can
feel tensions or maybe even pain.

Then you go to your abdomen,

Slowly up the thoracic spine, vertebrae for vertebrae.

You go up your back until you finally reach the shoulder area.

Now, consciously relax your shoulders by pushing them slightly downwards.

Now direct your attention to your cervical spine and let deliberately go of all the burden of the day.

Now check again at which point your body has contact with the exercise-mat.

If it is still uncomfortable you now have the brief opportunity to put yourself into a more comfortable position.

It is an autumn warm day, the sun shines and warms your skin.

You walk in a wine growing area over meadows and fields.

You can feel alternating crackling foliage while walking,

hard roots and stones,

and soft moss under your feet.

Now hold on for a moment and listen to the silence and the soft chirping of the birds.

A gentle slope leads you now up through a small vineyard.

Once you have reached the top, you enjoy the breathtaking view of autumn colored forests.

Now breathe deeply and let the fresh, clean air flow into your lungs.

A few meters further you discover a small bench in the middle of the vineyard where you can relax and recover from the strains of the ascent.

Now enjoy the beauty of nature,

feel the sun on your skin,

and feel the light wind in your face.

I wonder if you can even sense the smell of soil and moss and the fragrance of the moist foliage a little in your nose.

When you've rested enough, you'll pick up a few juicy, sweet grapes and then go on, the way back.

Again you notice the soft moss,

the hard roots and stones

and the crackling foliage under your feet.

Full of new strength and energy you are now able to master all the ups and downs of everyday life.

You are taking a deep breath now.

You slowly move your toes.

You clinch your hands to fists.

You feel the need to gently stretch, stretch and stretch.

You are now vigorously moving your whole body.

And as soon as you've gotten back here,
you open your eyes again with a small smile on your lips.

Sound Meditation at the Fireplace

Tip: This meditation is particularly suitable in the cold season for a pleasantly tempered resting place or a mild bio-sauna.

I warmly welcome you today (evening) with our sound meditation "Fireplace".

In the following meditation, you will soon imagine a flickering chimney fire and enjoy the relaxing warmth that comes from it.

I will call you by the more personal first-name of yours to address your subconscious mind intensively and sustainably.

I wish you a lot of fun!

Take a comfortable position and then go into your body with all your attention.

Now feel a little inside of yourself, if somewhere inside is a tension or perhaps even a pain present.

Direct your breath to this zone.

Feel, how the whole tension and all the blockages in you will become ever lighter and lighter, with every breath.

And you notice how you gradually get deeper and deeper into a relaxed state.

Imagine, you have taken a long walk in the fresh air and now come into a room where a fire at an open fireplace burns.

You first hear the cracking and crackling of the burning wood.

Then you see the blazing flames which delight your eye, in yellow, orange and red hue.

You cannot get enough of it!

Fascinated you're watching the colorful play for a while.

A little later you notice how the pleasantly dry heat of the fire spreads rapidly throughout the room and inside yourself.

You are warm, pleasantly warm, and a gentle breeze caresses your skin right now.

(You can utilize a larger decoration fan!)

Gradually, you begin to sweat intensely.

You are happy about the cleansing and the positive effect that the sweating now has on your organism and on your whole health.

Then, at your next shower, imagine that all of your blockages have dissolved in your body during this meditation and that the warm water spurt will also wash away all the burdening from you.

Soon it will be time to return with the thoughts into the present...

1. You are starting to move gently now.

2. Your movements become more intense.

3. You take a deep breath.

4. You open your eyes.

5. You have wholly come back here and feel refreshed and very comfortable.

Magic of Christmas

I sincerely welcome you to our Christmas meditation, which will remind you of a magical moment from the past.

Just try to turn the time a little back and watch the exciting and mysterious Christmas season again with children's eyes.

I will address you by your first-names, so to get a more intensive contact with you and your subconscious mind.

Take a pleasant and comfortable position on your exercise-mat and then go with your thoughts and your attention into your inner being.

Now concentrate on your breathing and feel how delightfully warm air flows into your body - and how it leaves, gently and without pressure.

You breathe perfectly calmly, placidly and evenly, at your own pace.

Soon you will inhale and then sink with each breath deeper and deeper into a comfortable and relaxed state.

It can be quite normal that you may still have everyday thoughts on your mind...

Let them simply come, unbiased, and go again - until there's nothing that can disturb you anymore in your peace and relaxation.

Now go back with your attention to your breathing rhythm.

Imagine how you travel a bit further into the past with every breath, until you finally arrive at a time you would like to remember.

Maybe you remember your sweet advent calendar with a little bit of chocolate behind every door.

And maybe, as you could hardly expect to open the next door every morning, to put the chocolate in your mouth...

Maybe there's also just high snow in your memory and you have built a beautiful snowman outside.

You come back to your home, drink a warm cup of tea, and then look out of the window at your snowman. You are just very content and happy at this moment…

Maybe you have also baked with your mother or grandma during the Advent cookies and always secretly nibbled a bit from dough.

Imagine the fine aroma that came out of the kitchen, and filled now all the rooms…

Maybe you have also created or bought a nice gift for someone who was especially close to your heart.

Now imagine again how you have given this person the gift and he/she was happy about it.

Maybe you are thinking about a Christmas market again.

You smell the sweet children's-punch and the tasty baked apple aroma.

You look with big eyes at the lighted booths with
their many beautiful, glittering and colorful things.

Maybe you remember the same as you on Christmas
Eve could hardly wait until it finally got dark…

How you have always discovered the gifts under the
Christmas tree!

How you unwrapped them impatiently and then
played the whole Christmas Eve with them,
and that you did not want to go to bed!

Maybe you can now take a little bit of this magic into
the pre-Christmas period and try again this year to see
the Christmas festival from a child's point of view.

I wish you a lot of joy and many wonderful moments!

And slowly it is time to return to the here and now.

Take another deep breath.

With each in- and exhale, you are now coming closer, one by one, back to the present.

You are also starting flexing your muscles from the top downwards.

First you clinch your hands into fists,

Then you will contract your stomach and back.

And lastly you flex your leg muscles.

You start to stretch, gently, easily.

You feel completely relaxed and when you are ready, you can open your eyes now!

Snowflake Meditation

Tip: The falling snowflakes with the B9-Kalimba from the "Hokema" company are particularly beautiful to display.

I would like to welcome you here in ... to our "Snowflake Meditation".

In the following approx. 20 minutes, you will experience a holistic relaxation for body, mind and soul.

To achieve a state of deep recovery, I will address you by your first-names.

You will now have a relaxed breath.

Feel how the breath gently flows in and out of your body.

How the belly is lifted - and lowered again.

You breathe completely calmly and at your own pace.

In and out.

In and out.

And now imagine you are on a winter evening in a small, quiet wooden hut high up in the mountains.

You sit comfortably in a rocking chair and a crackling fire burns in front of you in the open fireplace.

You drink a nice hot cup of tea, you are quite relaxed and you are pleasantly warm.

From your rocking chair you can see how it starts to snow again.

At first there are only very few small flakes, but after a few minutes, bigger, thicker flakes are already dancing past your window and slowly falling down from the sky to the ground.

You get up, stand by the pane and look at the beautiful crystals that fall down from the sky to the ground with no effort.
(Here possibly insert the Kalimba)

All of a sudden you are immersed in your thoughts and you are now transforming yourself into one of the small snowflakes.

You float weightlessly high up into the clouds, together with all the other snowflakes.

You dance and turn around with your friends full of energy and joie de vivre.

But gradually you become quieter and more relaxed, until you finally, as if carried by cotton wool, slowly and gently float down to earth.

And with every little bit you get closer to the ground, you sink deeper and deeper into a relaxed state.
(*Now again use the Kalimba*)

Happily smiling you now look completely overwhelmed down to the enchanted, white world.

The whole landscape looks like a white powdered sugar layer.

On the roofs is a warming snow-cover, surrounded by glittering icicles reflecting the warm light of the village.

In a garden is a large snowman with an orange carrot as nose.

Laughing children have left traces in the fresh snow with their sleds and skis.

I'll leave you a little time for your own winter pictures
(*Gentle play on the Kalimba*)

The cracking and crackling of the open fireplace brings your thoughts back to the small cabin, back to where our journey started.

You clinch your hands to fists.

You wiggle your toes.

You bring tension back into your whole body.

You start with slight movements.

You're stretching yourself entirely yet gently.

You are now back here, in the present.

You feel very comfortable and you are completely calm, placid and relaxed.

And whenever you see a snowflake or the color of white in the next time, your subconscious mind will return to this pleasant state.

„Dreamboat" – Pair - Meditation

Tip: Get a toy-megaphone and speak the words of the captain at the beginning. Play the Kalimba as and where indicated.

I welcome you today quite sincerely to our meditation. I've got (fitting for Valentine's Day) a pair-meditation prepared for you!

In case you're here alone, imagine that person that's closest to your heart, shall accompany you on your imaginary journey.

Please, breathe now a few times, intentionally, gently, tenderly,

in - and out,

in - and out,

in - and out...

Continue this soothing breathing technique throughout the meditation and feel how your thoughts slowly come to rest.

It is a beautiful and sunny day. We are now on a luxury steamboat in a large port.

(Possibly with megaphone):
"Attention, this is your captain speaking.
I'd like to welcome you on board of your dream ship, the 'Harmony'.
Please make yourselves comfortable and take a pleasant, relaxed position.
We'll leave the port in just another few minutes".

You stand with your partner on the deck of the luxury liner and watch the hustle and bustle in the harbor as the ship starts its powerful engines and gradually leaves the port.
(Maybe playing a melody with the Kalimba)

The sun is pleasant in the bright blue sky,
which warms your skin gently at this moment.

You are looking forward to the beautiful holiday ahead and the time that you will spend together.

A friendly waiter offers you a delicious welcome cocktail.

You stand at the rail and enjoy the beautiful view of
the lively harbor, which now gradually disappears
from your field of view.

The sea glistens in countless shades of blue,
and the sun is reflected in the water of the ship's pool.

Everything on the deck beams, shines and sparkles in
the sunshine.

You look happy, and at that moment you just enjoy
the free time and the each other's proximity.
Relaxation and some rest determines your further
day.

Now you have enough time to look around the ship a
bit,
or lay in the sun,
or take a refreshing swim in the pool,
just before the captain asks you for the candlelight
dinner later.

The harmonious tones and vibrations of the singing
bowls will now gently carry you and accompany your
thoughts.

Now it's slowing getting dark.

You can enjoy the incredible play of hues of a stunning sunset, which is only so at sea.

Soon after, the time has come to get dressed for the Captains' dinner.

Amazed you are while stepping into the dining room.

It is lit only by countless candles and is dipped completely in soft and warm colors.

You are now being served a delicious 5-course menu by a nice waiter.

First, everyone gets a small starter,

then a delicious soup,

now a tasty salad variation,

and now the very nicely dressed main dish.

Perhaps you can feel the taste of the delights even on your tongue?

In the end, several white-dressed waiters carry a sparkling ice cream buffet.

After this excellent meal you'd like to go for a stroll on board.

A breathtaking sight is offered to you:
The moon and millions of stars are mirrored on the surface of the water.

In the distance, you can discover a yellow-green-red weather light, which looks similar to the polar light.

You are completely speechless and overwhelmed by this beautiful natural drama and enjoy,
silent and happy, this unique sight!

Take in now these beautiful feelings of intense calmness, deep happiness and complete satisfaction.

Take it into your everyday life and try to find more time for each other.

Start right now, or tomorrow!

I wish you a wonderful,

harmonious future together!

(Possibly playing a melody again with the Kalimba)

It is time to say good-bye to this beautiful cruise on "Harmony" and to return with your mind to the here and now.

Take a deep breath now.

With every inhaling and exhaling, you become more aware of your surroundings.

Start gently to stretch.

After a few breaths you are then ready to open your eyes again.

(Possibly playing a final melody with the Kalimba)

Magic Moments

I welcome you here to Meditation of Magic Moments.

As you may know, the familiar first-name is usually used in meditations to get you into a deeper state of relaxation, so I'll address you by your first-names.

I wish you a lot of fun and nice experiences with the "magical moments".

Now take a relaxed breath and feel how you will come to rest more and more with each breath.

Go into your inner self with your thoughts and hear your heart beating, calmly and evenly.

How your breath mindful and gently flows in and out.

Everything what burdens you at this moment and all the things that may go through your head will become completely unimportant and fall off you at this moment.

You can feel how body, mind and soul are more and more merge into a unity.

In you it becomes quite still.

Everything in you will rest.

And now you go back in your mind to a magical moment in your life,
at a time,
in which you were full of energy and joy of life,
and you felt very content and happy.

Perhaps you have just experienced something great,
spent somewhere a great holiday,
or have finally reached your goal.

Perhaps you have also spent this very special moment in your life with a dear human being?

Certainly now comes something to mind,
a time you gladly remember.

If you want, put your hands over your chest or your lap and try to remember this positive situation again.

Remember exactly the circumstances of this magical moment,
of everything you felt,
have spoken or done.

Remember also exactly your feelings,
the environment,
the sounds
and all other details.

With all these beautiful thoughts, you even begin to smile a little...

And always then when in the next few days you are folding your hands in front of your body,
your subconscious mind can also remember exactly this jauntily and deep state of happiness,
energy and joy of life.

Now, for the last time,
take a relaxed breath,
and then, with all your attention,
slowly return to your normal breathing-rhythm.

Now, loosen the hands, and then flex the whole arm muscles, starting from the bottom to the top.

Then move your feet and contract them, starting from the bottom to the top.

Now move your entire body and start stretching.

And if you want, you may open your eyes.

You are back in the here and now.

You feel refreshed, very comfortable,
carefree and balanced and smile toward the rest of the day.

I hope you have been able to recall a magical moment of your life during our meditation and are now well recovered.

Moments of Happiness

I warmly welcome you to our meditation.

In the next 20 minutes you will feel like you are getting more and more calm and relaxing moments of happiness.

I wish you some nice experiences!

To achieve a state of deep recovery, allow me please that I address you by your first-names.

Close your eyes now and begin to breathe deeply into your abdomen, consciously and mindfully.

Just take notice how the breathing air flows in and out completely automatically without any effort.

As the breath lifts the belly - and lowers it again,
very easy,
very soft,
at your own pace.

The breath flows into your abdomen and
into your chest,

rises and lowers over and over again,
very soft,
very easy,
at your own pace.

Discern your inner rhythm consciously for a few
breaths.

Everything in you now has the chance to rest,
everything will be unimportant to you,
indifferent,
completely of no matter.

You are with the thoughts only with you.
And you feel as if more and more peace and evenness
in you want to spread.

All the stress of everyday life,
all tension
and all superfluous thoughts fade away,
become gradually less and less.

You only enjoy the silence,
the tranquility
and harmony.
And now, you've arrived at yourself.

Imagine you are sitting in the early morning hours on a beautiful meadow, high up on a mountain.

The sun rises slowly and is already to see over the distant peaks.

She is warming you now - with her gentle rays.

This very special atmosphere enhances the inner calmness and deep serenity in you.

You have left behind down in the valley,
while ascending the mountain,
with every step -
all the hustle,
all tension,
all stress.

All this is infinitely far away...

You let gently roam your eyes over the meadows, mountains and valleys.

You can enjoy the fresh mountain meadow air
and perhaps you can even get the spicy scent of the flowers and grasses wetted by the dew
easily perceive in your nose?

You're just very happy right now!

You are intensely enjoying this beautiful moment of deep happiness,
absolute relaxation
and infinite freedom.

And suddenly you begin to smile with joy.

Try to store this strong feeling deep inside you,
so that you can always fall back on it -
even in difficult situations.

Now take a last relaxing breath.

Let your breathing rhythm become stronger and stronger again.

Clinch your hands gently to fists.

Then move your toes gently.

Become more conscious of your whole body.

Make a few slight stretches and then make them more intense.

When you are ready, you finally open your eyes again.

Star - Magic

I welcome you warmly to our meditation „Star-magic".

Let for the next ca. 20 minutes body, spirit and soul slowly come to rest.

Enjoy deep inner recovery, and recharge your batteries with new strength and energy.

I wish you a nice rest!

During meditation, I will address you by your first-names to bring about a deeper relaxation.

Make yourself comfy on your exercise-mat,
feel then purposely into your own breathing rhythm.

You only pay attention to your breath,
feel how the chest lifts and lowers,
the air flows in and out,
in complete peace and harmony.

Now go with your thoughts somewhere to a beautiful
beach and lie down there in the evening sun.

You feel the warm sand under your body and
gradually notice how all the tension and stress from
your muscles and your entire body want to loosen...

You just enjoy this moment,
the here and now.

Gradually, the sun disappears behind the horizon and
poe a poe,
darkness of the night breaks in.

Above you, millions and billions of stars sparkle.

It is a breathtaking sight that makes you totally
overwhelmed and speechless.

Everything that burdens you,
all daily-life issues which go through your head,
it all becomes completely unimportant and lies now
very far away, left behind you.

You are now in the middle of your inner self and nothing can disturb you in your deep relaxation.

From afar you hear the soft rustling of the sea.

Every wave the sea washes to the beach brings you more and more recovery and deep relaxation.

The sand's warmth still heats your body and you feel completely comfortable, and wholly relaxed.

You look up again to the heavenly firmament and to the millions of stars that are light-years away from you.

At the sight of these stars, you suddenly feel how unimportant your own problems are in comparison to the vastness of the extent of the infinite universe.

And maybe you can now let go of some of it easier by now.

At the night-sky you observe how suddenly a shooting star falls from the sky -

and you can now,
exactly at this moment,
wish something.

If you really believe in it, this wish will surely be fulfilled soon.

Slowly release yourself from the sight of the starry sky and then go back into your body with your attention.

Pay more attention to your breathing.

Slowly adjust your breathing rhythm to normality.

Take a deep breath now.

Spread your fingers at the next breath.

Stretch during the next breath your legs out.

Bring tension into your entire body at the next breath.

And when you are ready, open your eyes again.

Dream of Hawaii

Tip: Hawaiian music, downloadable at Amazon
Song 1: Kealii Reichel, E O May,
Song 2: Kealii Reichel, Malie's Song, Hawaiian Lullaby,
Song 3: Kealii Reichel, Lei Hali`a,
Song 4: Kealii Reichel, Ku`u Pua Mae`ole

I warmly welcome you to our meditation.
In the next 30 minutes you will feel how body, mind and soul more and more come to calmness to the sounds of the singing bowls (and to traditional Hawaiian music).

I wish you a lot of fun!

To attain a deeper state of relaxation I'll address you by your first-names.

Close your eyes and let your thoughts calm down with each breath.

Then go with your whole attention into your body.

Breathe a few times quietly and gently in and out.

Become aware of where your body makes contact to the mat you're on.

Now go with your whole attention at your feet.

How do the heels feel?

And how your toes?

And how is the arch of the foot at this moment?

Notice it all unbiasedly.

And then walk slowly upwards -

over your calves,

onto your knees,

over the thighs,

up into the hips.

Concentrate now on your pelvis,

then on the belly.

Go up from the lower end of the spine,

up to the chest region,

and high into the cervical spine.

Lastly, feel into your fingers,

into the hands,

into your arms,

and then go over the elbows,

high up to the shoulders and then let them - deliberately and relaxed - fall.

Now concentrate on your head.

Take into account all the thoughts and potential tensions that may still concern you and let them go.

You have now arrived with your whole mindfulness in your inner center, and you fly mentally so relaxed, over Europe,

over the Atlantic Ocean,

over America,

then to the Pacific Ocean,

to the Islands of Hawaii.
(Music song 1: Kealii Reichel, E O Mai, briefly play, then fade out)

A bright blue sky and snow-white, infinitely long and palm-lined beaches await you already.
(Music Song 1: Kealii Reichel, E O Mai, speak, fade in, continue)

From a distance sounds, very quiet, (Hawaiian) music and the soft sounds of the singing bowls (and ukuleles) bring more and more peace and relaxation into your entire body.
(Music song 1: Kealii Reichel, E O Mai, fade out – speak text - then let music continue)

Thoughtfully now sit at this lonely beach and enjoy the breathtaking view of the sea.
(Music song 1: Kealii Reichel, E O Mai, fade out – speak text - then let music continue)

Inhale the fresh air deep into yourself.
(Music song 1: Kealii Reichel, E O Mai, fade out – speak text - then let music continue)

Feel the warmth of the sunrays on your skin.
(Music song 1: Kealii Reichel, E O Mai, fade out – speak text - then let music continue)

You let your spirit run free…..…

(Music song 1: Kealii Reichel, E O Mai, fade out – speak text - then let music continue)

Now enjoy the happiness of the moment very intensely, and absolutely nothing can disturb your deep relaxation now!
(Music song 1: Kealii Reichel, E O Mai, fade out – speak text - then let music continue)

(Song 2: Kealii Reichel, Malie's song, Hawaiian Lullaby, briefly play, then fade out)
After a while, however, you want to see where this beautiful music comes from.

You walk slowly a little down, in that direction – and you see a pair of dark-skinned, long-haired dancers in light-brown bast-skirts,
who perform the traditional Hawaiian Hula-dance.
(Song 2: Kealii Reichel, Malie's song, Hawaiian Lullaby, briefly play, then fade out)

One of the ladies has discovered you right away. She breaks from the group and comes to you with a friendly smile.
(Song 2: Kealii Reichel, Malie's song, Hawaiian Lullaby, briefly play, then fade out)

She welcomes you and puts her Lei (garland of flowers) around your neck.

(Song 2: Kealii Reichel, Malie's song, Hawaiian Lullaby, briefly play, then fade out)

She gives you to understand that you can now make yourself comfortable in a hammock between two palm trees.
(Song 2: Kealii Reichel, Malie's song, Hawaiian Lullaby, briefly play, then fade out)

A young man hands you a coconut filled with delicious liquid and while you enjoy your cocktail, you close your eyes and just take the relaxation, peace and harmony in your whole body.
(Song 2: Kealii Reichel, Malie's song, Hawaiian Lullaby, briefly play, let song finish)

(Song 3: Kealii Reichel, Lei Hali`a, briefly play, in-between texts to speak, continue)
You smile happily and enjoy the slightly sweet smell of the flowers in your nose,

you feel the fruity taste of the cocktail on your tongue,
(Song 3: Kealii Reichel, Lei Hali`a, briefly play, in-between texts to speak, continue)

 the pleasant warmth on your skin, *(Song 3: Kealii Reichel, Lei Hali`a, briefly play, in-between texts to speak, continue)*

the soft music in your ears
(Song 3: Kealii Reichel, Lei Hali`a, briefly play, in-between texts to speak, continue)

and you just feel great!
(Song 3: Kealii Reichel, Lei Hali`a, briefly play, in-between texts to speak, continue)

You dream along for a while, filled by feelings of harmony and happiness...
(Song 3: Kealii Reichel, Lei Hali`a, briefly play, in-between texts to speak, continue to its end)

(Song 4: Kealii Reichel, Ku`u Pua Mae`ole, briefly play, in-between texts to speak, continue)
But soon the time has come to mentally say Aloha to the pretty hours in Hawaii,
and to adjust back to reality.
(Song 4: Kealii Reichel, Ku`u Pua Mae`ole, briefly play, in-between texts to speak, continue)

Thankfully you send a last smile on your face,
just before you take a deep breath and slowly return into the here and now.
(Song 4: Kealii Reichel, Ku`u Pua Mae`ole, briefly play, in-between texts to speak, continue to its end)

Become aware of your feet and legs and start moving
them easily.

Next you direct your consciousness to your arms.

You gently move your hands and then both arms.

You start stretching now and if you want,
you now can open your eyes slowly.

Discover Your Inner Beauty

Welcome to our meditation: "Discover Your Inner Beauty".

In order to achieve your sub-consciousness even more intensively and more sustainably,
I will address you in our meditation all by your first-names.

If it is possible, please sit comfortably on your exercise-mat and erect yourself up straight.
If you want to lie down, just try to bring some length into your body.

Imagine an invisible thread pulls you gently and gives you sufficient support and strength.

Your body is still completely relaxed and radiates from the inside outwards extraordinary calmness and serenity.

Intently pay attention to your feelings.

Start at your feet and then go,
slowly,
bit by bit,
further up the body.

If, during your journey through the body,
you experience some tension or maybe even pain,
just send your breath right there.

And you can feel how, more and more,
ease and relaxation gradually spread there.

Now concentrate on your entire body.

Go to all the places that you find beautiful on you
and which ones you particularly like.

At this moment, however, be aware of the fact that
there is nowhere a perfect person and a completely
perfect body.

Everyone has places in oneself,
which one may not find so beautiful,
but which often seem unimportant to other people.

Each person is perfect in one's own way,
every human body has always something beautiful in
itself.

Perhaps this is sometimes not immediately apparent at first sight.

Perhaps your beauty is also hidden inside, waiting for you to be discovered and lived by you.

Now give yourself a smile and take the words "harmony" and "inner beauty" deeply into you while inhaling.

You breathe "harmony" and "inner beauty" into you.

Breathe still a few breaths independently.

Now fill your entire body with this harmony and beauty.

Feel how more and more satisfaction and self-confidence grow within yourself, by every breath.

You are a very wonderful person with many positive qualities that you can radiate from the inside out, in this moment,
but also in the future.

And now slowly get ready to return with the thoughts, back to the starting point of our small trip.

5 You slowly bring back tension into your entire musculature.

4 You start with slight movements.

3 Your movements become more intense.

2 You stretch gently.

1 And now you open your eyes,
 and you still have that inner smile on your face.

Dutch Sea of Tulips

I'd like to welcome you to our spring meditation.
Enjoy the invigorating effect and the fine fragrance of
colorful tulips in the following 30 minutes.
Recharge your batteries, calm your mind, and clear
your thoughts.

I wish you a lot of fun and a nice rest.

In order to reach a state of deep relaxation,
I'll now address you directly by your first-names.

Now take a comfortable and natural position on your
exercise-mat and concentrate only on your breath-
flow and my voice.

You can feel your belly's ceiling completely relaxed
rises when you in -
and slightly lowered when exhale.

How you become calmer and more placid,
with every breath you take.

And everything around you becomes
increasingly unimportant...

With each breath your inner peace is calming down
and a deep rest now wants to spread in your entire
body.

The fine vibrations of the singing bowls now
gradually become more and more intense here in the
room and slowly, in the form of waves,
are approaching you more and more.

You feel by the harmonious sound gently borne,
lovingly wrapped,
and you are completely safe.

The gentle vibrations lead your thoughts out of this
space.

They lead you towards Holland
to a huge, colorful tulip field.

Your arms are now transformed into wings,
and you now float quite lightly and uninhibited,
like a great butterfly on its gentle wings,
over a fragrant, colorful sea of flowers.

You feel an unprecedented joy and ease and just enjoy
this beautiful and carefree condition.

A gentle breeze blows a sweet flower-borne air to you
and lets you sink even deeper and deeper
into relaxation.

You float with your delicate wings over countless
tulips for a while,
until lastly,
you'll, very careful – land on a particularly beautiful,
red bloom.

Instantly you can feel the intense warmth of the
bright red color first in your feet
and then also in the rest of the body.

This red gives you powerful dynamics and energy,
that you can now absorb deeply into yourself.

After a while you have collected enough energy and
would like to visit another flower color.

Your graceful wings now carry you a little further
over the tulip field with footloose ease,
and this time you are looking for a sunflower-yellow
blossom.

This intense yellow gives you a great lightness and a new joy of life.

You start to shine with happiness, until you have a little smile in your face.

And again, you can absorb these beautiful feelings that this color triggers deep into you.

After some time you have collected enough feelings of happiness and again feel the inner need to change the color again.

You float, lightly and lightheartedly,
over the large, colorful tulip sea.
Full of grace,
carried by the tepid spring breeze,
in search of the next color.

You see many beautiful flowers and decide this time however for the color white.

The white soothes your mind,
clears your thoughts,
gives you quiet, inner peace and balance.
You have now arrived in your inner self's middle!

Happy and satisfied, you enjoy for a last time the
feeling of the carefreeness and ease that the butterfly
and the beautiful colors have given you.

In complete harmony, you now end this mental
journey with a deep breath,
and gradually begin to return.

Now you clench your hands to fists.

You start with little, gentle movements.

You bring back tension into your body.

You stretch yourself,
and then open,
if you are ready,
1
2
3
your eyes again.

And whenever you are longing for a rest,
you can reach this relaxed state again by consciously
using the colors red, yellow or white
through your subconscious mind.

We Embrace Spring

Feeling the first rays of sunshine on our skin after the cold season makes us much more comfortable and we feel the new awakening energy of life particularly intensive.

This very special feeling is our present meditation: "We Embrace Spring".

I will address you by your first-names and wish you, for the next approximately 20 minutes, a wonderful time out from everyday life!

While meditating, be aware of your breath
and feel it softly flows in you
and out again.
In and out.
In and out.

Imagine walking on a nice and warm spring-day a little outdoors.

The first, gentle sun rays warm your skin and you feel really comfortable.

Your path leads you over a small, narrow path to a green meadow.

The first flowers bloom there already.
You discover some small white daisies and yellow dandelion. (Or: yellow Easter bells)
On the trees are already delicate, green leaflets to be recognized, and the air smells completely of the beginning spring: fresh, sweet and aromatic.

You breathe this fragrance deeply in, and your inner energy increases with each breath more and more.

After a short while you feel
like as if you can tear down trees!

But soon you want to continue your walk and walk on the narrow, stony path that leads you to a small pond after a short time.

You discover a wooden bench where you can relax and recover from everyday life.

Your glances glide over the lake.

On the lake-shore yellow reed grows, and thin, green grass,
which gently flows to the rhythm of your breath
back and forth.

Back and forth again.
A duck-mother swims with her young chicks past you.

Their gentle movements curl the surface of the water into small, soft waves which are spreading more and more over the calm water level.

All your thoughts, everything else what preoccupies you, all this, slowly dissolves with the waves more and more.

The longer you observe this, the more peaceful your inner being becomes.

In you are soon only deep relaxation and great inner balance.

You savor this intense condition and feel yourself like a profound water that nothing, absolutely nothing, can now ruffle you.

Notice this harmonic state very clearly in you.

Try to store this feeling deep within you, so you can always recall of it in stressful situations.

Let your thoughts slowly return to the smooth water surface of the lake, and then, very gradually, return from your inner journey.

Your eyes remain closed at first.

Now, take a deep breath.

Then spread your fingers
and form a fist with your hands.

Next you wiggle your toes.

Now you move your whole body.
First only a little,
then the movements become more intense.

Now you are stretching until you are again,
bright and full of energy,
have fully arrived here in the present.

I hope you could clearly perceive your inner feelings
and you are now really well recovered and relaxed.

If it was your first meditation and the switching off
has not worked so well at first time, well -
I hope you will find the next days a little time
for a walk outside in Mother Nature…

Enchanting Spring Awakening

After the cold winter months and the darkness
every human being has the inner need for
warmth, sun and nature.
This is what's this meditation's about.
I wish you lots of fun for the next half hour.

As you probably know, in meditations the
participants, are usually addressed by their first-names
so that a deeper relaxation is achieved.
I will do the same for you.

Imagine, you are on a beautiful spring-day
somewhere outside in nature and
enjoy the first warm sun rays on your skin.

The warmth feels good, and you feel well
and nothing can disturb you in your good mood.

Everything that is burdening you in your everyday life,
all you still may have to do,
all this now will be completely indifferent to you.

You let your eyes wander over the landscape.

Nature awakens,
the first snowbell- and -flake flowers stretch their
heads through the last snow
and greet the spring with joy.

They have recently pushed themselves with their
whole force through the ground.

Now they are gently rolling in the tepid wind,
back and forth.

Just as gentle as your breath now flows,
in and out.

Your breath gently flows
in and out,
in and out.

The winter has cost you a lot of energy
and it is now time to refuel yourself with new one.

Soon you will feel this dynamic very intensely in you.

The whole environment, the whole nature, is once
more, like you, tuned to growth and renewal.

The lightness of spring brings new impetus to you.

Perhaps you are looking for a healthier diet,
more exercise in the fresh air or even
starting something new?

Now is the right time for this!
You are going to walk a bit.

You can observe everywhere the growth and the
change in nature.

Take a closer look:
fresh and delicate green in different tones
sprouts on the trees and shrubs.

Red tulips,
yellow daffodils,
purple grape hyacinths
and many other spring flowers are already lighting up
toward you from far away.

All these colors delight your inner being and
everything in you also begins to radiate happily.

This inner smile would like soon to spread over on
your face.

You enjoy the warm spring breeze,
which gently caresses your skin,
the fine flowery air,
your nose flattering.

You take an intense breath that gives you new energy
and freshness.

And the longer you breathe in this spring air,
the deeper you fall into a
completely comfortable and relaxed state.

The migrating birds have returned from their winter
quarters and are already welcoming you in the early
morning hours with their cheerful songs.

The humming of the bees and the chirping of the
birds sound like music in your ears.

From afar a dog barks and you hear untroubled child
laughs.

A small squirrel climbs down from the tree and
searches the ground for the last nuts that it has
hidden there in autumn.

Two large white swans swim majestically across a lake
and also a few small fish jumping full of joy from the
water.

You too will now be struck by this joy of life,
the energy, the unprecedented energy, and the new
beginning that nature now provides for you.
Let this mood have a few moments
for taking affect on you.

The chirping of the birds now brings you back from
your thoughts into the present.

Take a deep breath.

With every in- and exhaling,
freshness and energy enter your body.

You move your fingers and make them to fists.

You are stretching, out, towards the sun.

You've come back to the room again fully awake
- and, with a smile –
you will welcome this beautiful spring day.

Indian Nights

Tip: It is particularly nice if you'd hand out before the meditation to each participant a tea bag with Indian herb-tea or a cotton-pad dubbed with clove oil, which then can be placed on the chest.

I am glad welcoming your visit to our common time-out.

I will address you during the guided meditation in the following approximately 20 minutes by your first-names to give you a deeper level of relaxation.

So try to leave everyday life out of the box and really use that time here very consciously.

Seek now for a position that is comfortable for you and then close,
when you are ready,
your eyes.

Now concentrate on your breathing and feel the slow flow of the air,
which gently flows in and out of your body,
for a few seconds.

With every breath you feel more and more the peace
and serenity in your inner being.
Now imagine a journey, a journey that will
bestow you with deep relaxation.

You are now in India at a spice market.

The most diverse colors and fragrances
flatter your eyes and your nose.

The spicy scent of brown tangy cloves,

of yellow curry

and fresh green pepper.

These fragrances stimulate your mind and sharpen
your senses.

You take these fragrances deep into you now.

From far away you can hear softly, typically Indian
music and cheerful people talk, laugh and sing.

Curiously you now walk into this direction and
discover in a large building by an open window

some Indian dancers barefoot in their colorful saris,
singing, laughing and dancing.

Somebody is waving to you and invites you to attend
the feast too.

You are pleased accepting this invitation and then
observe the joyous events.

One after another, all the people in the room get up
and join the dancing women, until hardly anyone sits
in his place.

Maybe you even want to dance a little with them?

Time flies by and it's been getting dark.

The joyous festival is now approaching its peak.

Countless colorful lights are being lit
and sweet smelling lotus flowers
are given to each participant.

All the people now go outside and run,
Singing, laughing and dancing in a kind of procession
towards the River Ganges.

Then there, the colorful lanterns are put into the
water.

After that, each one puts his lotus-flower carefully
into the source of life and leaves it, connected with
the beautiful desire for the future,
mindfully and slowly driving away.

You'll still follow your flower with your eyes,
until you cannot see it anymore.

Then it gradually becomes quieter
and soon you can only hear
the soft rippling of the water.

You now enjoy this peace and sink deep
into relaxation.

Gradually, however, it is time to say good-bye
to your wish and also to India
to return slowly to the present.

Take a deep breath,
clinch your hands to fists,
move your arms and legs.
And then - stretch yourself, prolonging.

Than enjoy your rest of the day!

In the Land of the Pharaohs

Tip: Offer, after this meditation, refreshing peppermint tea, depending on the season, warm or cold!

I welcome you cordially.

We are going to travel to Egypt, to the land of the pharaohs.
Let yourself be enchanted and enjoy this very special oriental atmosphere.

For the next, about 20 minutes, I wish you a nice rest and experience!

During meditation I will address you by the more personal first-name of yours, to keep you and your subconscious awareness more sustainably.

As always, meditation will only take you as far as you need to relax.

It is a beautiful, warm summer day and your today's journey of relaxation starts in the distant Egypt.

Outside of town, a group of Bedouins with their peaceful camels awaiting their guests.

They welcome you with a drink.

One of the camels looks kindly at you
with his soft, brown eyes and you feel attractet to it.

It lowers the head and goes to its knees before you.

Full of expectation, you sit on its back.

Soon every rider has found his camel and slowly
the caravan is moving leisurely.

You feel safe and secure, and the soothing, gentle
rocking of the animal will soon lead you into a state
of deep relaxation.

In the distance a pyramid dilatorily emerges, and you
look fascinated, as you come closer and closer.

With each step of your camel, the monument
becomes bigger and bigger.

Completely overwhelmed you the sight of this
gigantic structure take effect on you.

After a while, the caravan starts moving again and the familiar rocking and waving of your camel helps you return to the necessary inner peace and serenity.

Around you is now nothing but sand, pleasant warmth and a bright blue sky.

You enjoy this moment as intensely as possible and feel safe and secure.

On the horizon there's a small, green spot visible and the caravan moves leisurely in this direction.

Gradually the first green palms and several white Bedouin-tents become visible.

In the oasis life spurts, there is lively event.

It is a huge contrast to the uniform color and dryness of the desert.

You are warmly and kindly received, a selection of beverages is ready for you.

On silver trays dried fruits as well as oriental treats and lukewarm,
fragrant peppermint tea are offered.

The most varied tastes flatter your taste buds.

Refreshing and strengthened you spend a wonderful evening with lovely people,
before the coolness of the night slowly irrupts.

In your mind let review the whole day,
before concluding happy and satisfied your inner journey.

And with the fading away of the singing bowls, it is now time to come slowly back to the here and now with the thoughts.

Now, with some deep breaths, let fresh air flow into your lungs.

Make a fist and spread your fingers.

Move your toes first and then the whole leg.

Stretch yourself now and smile happy,
toward the rest of the day.

Forest-walk: Oasis in Everyday-Life

Tip: Use a few drops of ethereal tannin oil to evaporate in a suspended scent lamp, so you can deepen the effect of meditation. Here I particularly recommend the CD "Birdsong without Music - Summer Day in the Forest" (= German Edition "Vogelgezwitscher ohne Musik – Sommertag im Wald") by Thomas Rettenmaier (Delta Music), ASIN: B003S5FQL2

I would like to warmly welcome you to our today's journey with the theme of "Forest-walk: "Oasis in Everyday-Life".

Whenever you need a little time out,
you can use the various impressions of nature to recharge your batteries with new energy and find your way back to your inner self.

However, if you are not able to do so due to lack of time,
simply let your mind wander and go for a relaxing walk…

I will now address you directly by your more personal first-names, to allow you a deeper relaxation.

Lay or sit comfortably,
and then close your eyes.

The next approximately 20 minutes now belong to you alone.

You have the certainty that you are doing something
good for yourself and your soul in the next minutes.

Feel in every breath how your muscles wanting to
relax more and more,
and everything in you will come to rest.

Let your thoughts come and go unbiasedly,
until you have arrived to your inner self.

Deep inside you,
you know that nothing is happening,
that shouldn't happen…

You will start thinking about a beautiful hike,
a relaxing walk that will take you to glittering creeks,
verdant forests and meadows.

It is a beautiful summer day,
the sun shines from the blue sky,
and you are pleasantly warm.

You will pass through a colorful flower meadow,
into a light-flooded forest.

The sun shines radiantly through the branches of the
trees and dips the clearing into gentle, warm colors.

You only hear your steady steps,
and the soft rustling of the leaves
which are swaying back and forth with the wind.

Your breath also flows gently back and forth,
in your own rhythm,
in and out,
back and forth,
in and out.

The quiet humming of the bees,
gathering the sweet nectar on the firs,
soothes your mind and your thoughts.

You are now walking a few steps through this
enchanted section of nature,
and then,
somewhere,
lie in the soft, dense moss.

The pleasant, spicy scent of various woods, grasses
and mushrooms will soon make you sink into a state
of deep relaxation.

You only hear the soothing sounds of nature and with
the increasing outer silence you can also gradually feel
and perceive your inner being.

In you is a soothing calmness and deep serenity.

After a short time, your looks will be relaxed.

You can see some white clouds that pass by you.

Then you see a few birds, who, happily chirping,
flying from branch to branch.

At some distance graze a few shy deer,
which now slowly trot towards you.

They only stand a few meters in front of you and then
eat the lush, green grass quietly.

You can now observe them very closely:
their gentle brown eyes,
the slender, wiry body,
the light brown fur
and - the imposing antlers.

You are quite fascinated by the beauty of these
animals you have never seen so close in the wild.

A woodpecker suddenly breaks the silence with his
pecking, and the deer quickly seek for the expanse.
You too rise from your soft ground, and continue
your way, heedful, until you reach a very different part
of the forest.

In the meantime you feel very balanced and sense that outer silence and harmony have now spread completely within you.

You're enjoying the sight of light green grasses, of strong green foliage-trees, and you see many brown cones dangling from the deep, dark green branches of the tall spruces.

Your path leads you then over a slight hill and you can see behind it a small stream, sparkling and glittering in the sunlight.

The cool water flows quietly and evenly, and always finds its way past stones, plants and fallen branches.

It masters every obstacle and flows around all what is in its way, gently and calmly.

You watch it for a while...

Soon you realize that, just as the water is paving its way through nature, you too will find your right way through life with the necessary calmness and prudence.

The refreshing walk is now slowly coming to an end, and with the fading away of the last tone, it will be time to return, gradually back to the here and now.

Take a deep breath.

With every inhaling and exhaling, you will become more and more awake and alert.

Now lump your hands to fists.

Start with gentle movements.

Make your movements more intense.

Stretch yourself now.

And with a relaxed smile on your face you open your eyes and intentionally enjoy the rest of your remaining day.

The Tree of Life

I warmly welcome you to our today's meditation "The Tree of Life"

Our whole life is characterized by different stages of development, of inner and outer growth.
For this we need a strong soil attachment, a stable stand and a deep rooting in the earth.

This meditation will be just about that for the next 20 minutes.

During meditation, I will also address you directly by your first-names in order to be able to reach your subconscious even better.

I wish you lots of fun and nice insights.

Now take a comfy position on your mat.
You can sit or lie down, just as you wish.

Now breathe a few breaths of air consciously into your lungs, gently, and - again.

Feel exactly what happens in you.

As your belly rises,
and lowers again.

How the air flows into you -
and how it leaves you again.

Now imagine you are a small chestnut and lie
below a large chestnut tree.

One day a small child comes by and pick up you
laughing from the ground,
plays a little with you and throws you,
somewhere and -how,
onto a large meadow…

And there are ideal conditions for you:
fertile soil and bright light.
The heat of the sun's rays
and alternately also some rain -
all in a harmonious combination.

You lie on the ground for a while,
and then you feel ever more intensely the strength of
your inner growth,
the desire of personal development.

Your outer shell begins to show cracks,
and the strong seed in you is now seeking its way
down into the warm,
fertile earth.

Gradually, many deep roots develop,
the foundation on which a large,
strong tree can slowly build.

Soon a small, green sprout also grows upwards,
high up,
toward the sunlight.

The first, delicate leaves are then formed.

And gradually you also grow small twigs,
all once becoming large,
strong branches…

Earth nourishes you,
the sun warms you,
the rain replenishes you,
and the wind rocks you gently back and forth.

You give yourself to all this,
full of confidence and with the inner certainty,
that nothing happens to you, that nothing is missing,
and Mother Nature has only the best in mind
with you.

So the years go by and you slowly grow to a little tree.

Your delicate bark is gradually getting harder.

You can, so well protected, defy any storm, wind,
rain, or even hail.

Your roots and branches are getting stronger and,
more and more, branching out.

You have gotten lots of sensors and antennas,
with which you sun,
water and food can absorb you deeply -
and thus convert into oxygen required for life
to your environment.

Your roots now reach deep into the fertile earth and
give you strong hold.

Your branches and leaves grow ever farther upwards,
they stretch out towards the Sun and thus give you
also outer freedom.

You have the feeling of being "borne" by safety, love
and the inner certainty, always to get all that you need
for yourself, your growth and your further
development.

In the course of the years you grow to a large, stately
tree.

You have seen many things and can also tell some
stories:
for example, children who have camped under you,

of young, in love couples,
who gave themselves the first kiss under you,

of innumerable animals, which you have given all the
years protection and shelter by rain and snow,

and from the lightning, which almost once
had stricken into you…

And one day a small child would come by and
pick up laughing one of your chestnuts from the
ground,
plays a little with it and throws it,
somewhere and -how,
onto a large meadow
and the chestnut falls back on fertile soil…

And so the cycle of the "tree of life" concludes.

Now prepare yourself slowly to let your deep roots
become your own feet again.

Your strong branches are forming back
into your arms.

The little branches turn into your fingers.

Nevertheless, you can still be deeply rooted to your mat you're on,
to the ground,
on which you will be firmly standing again later.

And you still intake the force, strength and energy of the big chestnut tree which now accompanies you through your life.

Return to the present with this certainty.

Now clinch your hands to fists.

Move your feet, first gentle, then stronger.

Stretch your hands upwards, towards the sky and push your feet slightly down.

Be happy about this day,
and then feel a bit more of it,
if you want to.

The Cave of the Sparkling Crystals

Today, I welcome you to our meditation "The Cave of Sparkling Crystals", where you can feel the power, energy and positive effects of the different precious stones.

Try to imagine everything well and experience a lasting, deep relaxation.

During the next 20 minutes, I will address you directly by your more personal first-names, that way to reach your sub-consciousness deeper.

Take a comfortable position, close your eyes, and then pay your whole attention to your breath.

Feel how you,
light and gentle,
breathe in and out,
how your body always wants to relax more and more.

Your abdomen convexes gently,
and then concaves slightly.

Breathe for a few more breaths at your own pace.

Imagine now you are on a hike in the mountains and have a heavy backpack.

The sun is shining from the sky and you have become very warm.

You want to take a break and look for a cool place.

You discover a small rock with a large opening that looks almost like a gate.

Bright light glows outwards.
You go inside, and suddenly you stand in a huge cave, full of sparkling crystals.

You look around, overwhelmed what treasures nature has produced here.

A sea of soothing colors appears before your mind's eye.

You are now immersed in a magical world:
everything shines, glitters and sparkles
in the colors of the rainbow.

Many types of crystals and precious stones can be found here:

Dark rubies, they stand for love and happiness.

Blue lapis lazuli, they give you self-confidence and a powerful voice.

Purple amethysts, they provide you with inner peace and serenity.

Green emeralds, you get from them self-healing power and harmony.

Yellow citrine, which gives you a sense of life and new courage.

White mountain crystals, the symbol of purity and clarity.

You can now select a property of the stones
and your favorite color,
or a color that attracts you.

Try to go through your body with your mind.

Start at the toes and then go slowly higher.

Where do you feel tensions?

Where do you have pain?

Where do you need your attention?

Let this symbiosis of color, energy and power of the gemstone flow precisely there.

Soon you will be able to feel the warmth and deep relaxation that will spread out,
more and more.

With every breath you take the effect of the color and the energy of the stone deep inside you and
while exhaling, simply relieve all burdensome.

It is getting lighter and lighter within you.

After being so physically relaxed,
you also want to free your mind and soul from unnecessary ballast.

You look around and see a big, brown crate
in the back of the cave.

You can now put the heavy backpack you have on your shoulders,
down on the ground.

It bears the name "Backpack of Life"
and contains all the situations
that currently concern you.

Now open this box and fill it with all the contents of your backpack.

Now pack everything,
bit by bit,
in there.

Then close the box by simply dropping the heavy lid down. So, nothing can come back to you again.

You can now feel the relief, now you feel a sense of lightness and indifference.

And now fill your empty backpack with precious memories,

with nice moments you have already experienced,

with inspiration and joy of life,

with happiness and new energy.

We now give this backpack the name
"Backpack of Happiness".

Now, get ready,
very slowly,
for the way to the outside.

Do not forget to take your "Backpack of Happiness" with you so that you can go back to the content whenever needed!

On the way back you fill the body, mind and soul with the colors and the effects of the crystals.

The closer you get to the exit the more your thoughts come back to the present.

Now clinch your hands to fists.

Then move your toes.

And, then stretch yourself.

Open, when you are ready, your eyes again.

I hope you could relax beautifully?

I wish that you can fill your
"Backpack of Happiness"
daily with many new, valuable moments.

I wish you lots of fun with the meditations!

Do you own a smartphone? Please use this QR code to get more information: (in German language)

Homepage for Dr. Edward Bach Flower Remedies
www.bluetenberatung.de

Homepage for Singing-Bowls
www.tibetische-klangschalen-massage.de

Facebook: "Bachblüten Klangschalen"

About the Internet shop you can find all my German and English published books of "Sound Massage With Singing Bowls Easy Done" and "Meditation Made Easy With Singing Bowls".

You will also find CDs and audio samples of my most beautiful meditations.

I am looking forward to your visit!

Translation: Georg Woodman, Dr. MSc., Dr. Phil., University CA/USA